MW01232953

BODY LANGUAGE SECRETS

Table of Contents

DISCLAIMER

Copyright © 2017

All Rights Reserved

No part of this book can be transmitted or reproduced in any form including print, electronic, photocopying, scanning, mechanical or recording without prior written permission from the author.

While the author has taken the utmost effort to ensure the accuracy of the written content, all readers are advised to follow information mentioned herein at their own risk. The author cannot be held responsible for any personal or commercial damage caused by information. All readers are encouraged to seek professional advice when needed.

About The Author

George Pain is an entrepreneur, author and business consultant. He specializes in setting up online businesses from scratch, investment income strategies and global mobility solutions. He has built several businesses from the ground up, and is excited to share his knowledge with readers. Here is a list of his books.

Books of George Pain

Importance of Body Language

Since ancient times, we have used our body language to communicate, conveying our emotions and thoughts to those around us. Each person out there has a different body language, encompassing not only facial expressions but also body postures and gestures. Even eye movement is considered as part of the non-verbal communication, being closely followed by touch and using one's personal space.

Body language, an integral element of non-verbal communication

As the above quote clearly points out, 80% of human communication is actually non-verbal. Some experts argue it may even be more. Body language is considered an integral element of non-verbal communication, being used, consciously or unconsciously, to interact with other people. It is often said that body language will serve to complement verbal communication. Through our gestures, postures and expressions, we are actually transmitting a lot of information about ourselves to the interlocutor.

It is clear that the body language can make the difference between a successful interaction and one that is doomed to fail from the start. Basically, the information transmitted through non-verbal means, will ensure proper interaction between two or more people. However, due to cultural differences and other influencing factors, it is important to state that body language can sometimes lead to confusion or a state of ambiguity. One has to be able to use his/her body language to his/her own advantage, working at the same time to decipher the non-verbal information transmitted by the other person with utmost accuracy. In the end, by mastering the art of non-verbal communication, you will have more successful interactions with other people; reducing the risk of misunderstandings, confusion and social awkwardness.

How important are facial expressions?

Each person on this planet has facial expressions, commonly used to express emotions and/or thoughts. It is amazing how many muscles are involved in these facial expressions, allowing us to express our happiness, sadness or anger. Our eyebrows go high when we are surprised. We wrinkle our noses when something does not suit our preferences. The corners of our mouths go up when we are happy. An avalanche of facial expressions deliver information to the interlocutor regarding the way we feel or think.

Interestingly enough, we often use facial and bodily expressions at the same time, in order to convey a more meaningful interpretation of our thoughts and feelings. The person receiving the information will analyze both facial and body expressions at once, using his/her body language to respond to the situation in question.

The body posture serves to communication tremendously

A person's body posture can provide information regarding the way he/she is feeling. It is also useful for determining what that person thinks, at the moment in question. Bodily postures serve as a reflection of our emotions, whether we are aware of this for a fact or not. For example, if a person is sitting on a chair, with the back relaxed and arms and legs open, this means he/she is indeed relaxed, interested in communicating with the person standing in front of him/her. On the other hand, if the arms and legs are crossed, the interest in the said interaction is very low, if non-existent.

Even the smallest gesture matters

A wise person once said that small gestures can have a big impact. Throughout the entire day, we interact with a number of people, using gestures to complement our verbal messages. Our arms, hands and fingers move in various directions, as well as our head and legs. Most of these gestures are involuntary, but voluntary gestures can be used to highlight information that has been transmitted through oral means.

The gestures that we make can have a different impact, depending on the culture to which we belong. For example, many of the finger gestures that are acceptable in Western cultures and offensive in the Middle East. It is always important to take your time and determine whether a gesture is acceptable from a cultural point of view or not.

You will ensure appropriate interaction with the other person, without running the risk of being culturally insensitive.

What kind of information can gestures deliver? Well, let's take the hand gestures as example. If your hands are relaxed and moving openly, this means that you have confidence in the information you are presented with, of course, in yourself (self-assurance). On the other hand, keeping your hands clenched can indicate that you are either stressed or angry. Constantly moving your hands or wringing them together can mean that you are agitated, nervous or anxious.

The Chemistry behind Body Language

Communication is essential for us as human beings. Most of the times, when we think about communication, we tend to focus on verbal communication. However, the reality is that non-verbal communication matters more. Just think about it. Humans have been using non-verbal communication since the dawn of time, long before the spoken language appeared.

Non-verbal communication tells us a lot about how we are and the message we are trying to convey. It communicates more information than actual words, especially in relation to the things we are feeling or thinking. In fact, numerous studies have confirmed that non-verbal communication delivers more meaning than any other form of communication.

We tend to rely on gestures and facial expressions, in situations where we are unsure about the verbal message we want to deliver. It has also been discovered that non-verbal communication is preferred for the expression of emotions and thoughts, even though this might actually occur involuntarily.

Let's look at an example. Imagine that someone asks you something but you are not certain about the intentions behind the said question. Well, in such a situation, you will most likely rely on non-verbal communication, in order to identify the emotions or thoughts of the person asking the question. The more interpersonal the interaction, the more you will rely on non-verbal cues for help. This is valid for emotional exchanges as well.

Perhaps the most interesting thing about non-verbal communication is that it almost always is involuntary. Given its nature, you cannot control just as easily as verbal communication and, most importantly, you cannot fake it. Not sure about that? Go back in time and remember meeting someone for the first time. If you did not like him/her, it is highly likely you've involuntarily sent non-verbal messages about your interest. It is difficult to fake interest, no matter how hard you might try.

You can look at non-verbal communication as the main factor for communicating your thoughts and feelings. While it is true that some people learn to control their gestures and facial expressions; they do so to achieve a particular objective. They are people who represent important companies, so they must educate themselves and deliver the messages of the company, without transmitting their own personal opinion through non-verbal cues. The rest of us have a hard time controlling our non-verbal attitude, especially when we get in a situation where personal thoughts and feelings have to be necessarily expressed.

Is non-verbal communication ambiguous?

Verbal communication is crystal clear, in majority of situations. Non-verbal communication, on the other hand, is quite ambiguous, with both facial expressions and gestures being given a multitude of meanings, depending on the situation at hand, cultures or personalities involved. There are many non-verbal cues that do not have a specific meaning, being open to interpretation. Sometimes, in order to reduce the level of ambiguity, we may rely on other clues, such as the environment we are in or the words spoken by our interlocutor.

And what about credibility?

When a person speaks on a subject, you are not necessarily inclined to believe him/her. In deciding whether the words spoken by that person are worth believing or not, you will probably take a multitude of factors into account, including his/her background, culture and experience in the field he/she is speaking about.

Amazingly enough, we find it easier to believe the information transmitted through non-verbal means. Peter Drucker once said that the most important thing in communication is hearing what isn't said. Well, non-verbal communication is much more credible than verbal message, mainly because it is difficult to be faked or kept under control.

Non-verbal communication often has an involuntary nature and this is one of the reasons why the messages transmitted through it present a higher level of credibility. Basically, you cannot fake your gestures or facial expressions, so the other person will respond in an honest and proper manner as well.

Non-verbal communication, reinforcing the way we feel/think

Many of the facial expressions that we use on a daily basis are involuntary. Our bodies have become accustomed to using these, as a way of reinforcing the way we feel and think. Sometimes, verbal communication is not enough to demonstrate to others our emotional state or the thoughts going through our mind. For example, let's say you want to tell a joke to a friend. By smiling, you will improve the quality of the communication, as your non-verbal cues will convey a clear message about the way you are feeling.

It is important to understand that non-verbal communication has a clear and deep impact on relationships. This impact can be either positive or negative, depending on the situation in which you find yourself into. We often rely on gestures, in order to express our emotions, especially when it comes to interactions with the ones we love or cherish. Friends hold hands, lovers kiss and mothers always caress their children. Non-verbal communication guarantees closer relationships, even when no verbal communication has taken place.

In today's modern world, we rely on verbal communication to identify the best solutions to existent problems. This type of communication might be used in order to receive/give detailed instructions about a task we have to handle. However, non-verbal communication remains an excellent method to convey our emotions and/or thoughts to others. It is efficient and, most importantly, it is always accurate. So, the next time you are at a loss for words, let your body do the talking for you. It is guaranteed it will do a job, telling the other person how you really feel or think.

Four distances in Body Language

Body language usually shows the extent of your feelings for someone. For instance, your feelings for another person, whether you like him or her as a friend or as a romantic interest, will show through your body language. Another important factor is the physical distance you observe from the person you are interacting with, since each relationship and social setting have their own recommended distance. Therefore, the next time you are in a conversation, take note of the distance you are keeping from someone. Your body language sends a stronger message than even the words that you are saying. People are very keen to read more into nonverbal signals than what comes out of the mouth.

To avoid being misunderstood, it is a good idea to learn about some of the common distances observed in nonverbal communication. You can then use the information you learn to nail your point home by sending the right message.

Intimate distance

With this distance, you are supposed to observe a difference of 6 to 18 inches with your partner. This distance is usually reserved only for people who are intimate and have a strong affection for each other. This distance is enough to allow for actual touching, meaning there is a bigger opportunity to be closer to each other. Couples usually observe this distance when they are in public.

If you are dealing with a person that is not connected to you intimately, make sure to keep the proper distance because invading someone's personal space can be a disturbing gesture and can make them feel uncomfortable. Intimate distance is preserved for people who have close relationships, such as lovers, close family members, or even well-adored pets. In these cases, keeping a smaller distance helps to strengthen existing bonds.

Personal distance

A distance of 1.5 to 4 feet is personal distance that is common between close friends and colleagues. You will always find people in deep conversation keeping this distance, especially as people are more able to observe their colleague or friend's body language. Expressions like movement of the eyes and lips send a very strong nonverbal message that shows the direction the conversation is going. It is very critical that the appropriate distance, based on the social setting, is strictly maintained.

If you want to shake hands, the personal distance is also appropriate, as it allows you enough space for this action, as well as any other physical gestures that you deem important in a casual social setting. This is due to the distance being able to cover the arm length, which is convenient when you are holding discussions as a group. You will not have any limitations to your movements, regardless of the number of people around you. There is enough space for your use and comfort is assured. Whenever you have associates and friends close to you for some discussions, ensure that you maintain a personal distance. When the appropriate personal distance is kept, people are more comfortable and at ease.

Social distance

This distance requires two people to be 4 to 12 feet away from each other. Since this distance is more for social meetings, there is no need to keep a further distance away, such as the one you would keep for formal settings. In these settings, remember to also respect the positioning of the other people around you. Your body language and where you choose to position yourself in a room has a significant effect on how you are perceived by others. It is important to send across a humble, non-dominating, appearance so other people in the meeting can feel like they are being respected and heard. In social meetings, every person should be given an equal opportunity to participate.

Social distance is designed in such a way that maintaining eye contact among the people present is easy. Speeches delivered at social meetings should also be loud enough so that everyone can hear. Having the right amount of eye contact and voice volume can help to make communication a success. Without these essential elements, the effectiveness and productivity of social meetings will be lowered.

An additional note is that some social meetings can also be formal as well. Thus, there are exceptions to the distance of 4 to 12 feet. Knowing which distance is appropriate in which situation is crucial.

Public distance

This distance measures 12 to 25 feet and comes into play in public meetings where one person is addressing a multitude. It is necessary to make sure the information being passed across can be received by all people without any exceptions. Additionally, at a public podium where the crowd may be more charged, this distance offers safety by shielding the speaker from possible attack. It is always good to keep a safe distance from people who might attack any time. However, considering the farther distance, public speakers standing 12 to 25 feet away from their audience are forced to mostly use exaggerated nonverbal gestures to effectively communicate their message to their audience. The speaker's message is most effective when his or her body language combines well with their spoken word.

At this distance, it will also be very difficult for the people to see the speaker's facial expressions. Thus, it becomes even more crucial for the speaker to effectively use gestures to add spark to his or her message. People who are experienced in public speaking and know how to read body languages will be very swift in making quick adjustments to suit their crowd or audience. For instance, experienced speakers will use larger hand or head gestures to substitute for their audience not being able to see their facial expressions at a far distance. Another example of someone who would keep a public distance is a teacher, who keeps a good space from students while teaching.

Now that you have learned about the different distances, you must choose the appropriate distance for the appropriate situation. Don't choose an intimate distance when you are speaking at a public gathering or vice versa. Understanding these nonverbal communication gestures will benefit you in many ways, whether it is personally or through your relationship with others. Understanding body language can help you better understand how other people are feeling in a situation. Being able to communicate good body language will also help you more effectively develop relationships, so others will take the time to know you and form a relationship with you.

A Short message from the Author:

Hey, are you enjoying the book? I'd love to hear your thoughts!

Many readers do not know how hard reviews are to come by, and how much they help an author.

I would be incredibly thankful if you could take just 60 seconds to write a brief review on Amazon, even if it's just a few sentences!

Please head to the product page, and leave a review as shown below.

Thank you for taking the time to share your thoughts!

Your review will genuinely make a difference for me and help gain exposure for my work.

Body Language Signals - Lower Limbs

If the person's legs are shoulder width apart, either when standing or in a seated position, it indicates that the person is relaxed.

Crossed legs

Crossed legs might be interpreted to mean somebody needs some privacy, thus he or she is completely closed up. Other people will have access to you denied, so there is no room to kick start any type of talk. The other messages that crossing legs could mean is that you are not ready to leave. You want to stay around for longer and get the assurance that nobody will kick you out. In men, crossing the legs can be used as a way of protecting masculinity. People who have low self-esteem are known to prefer this positioning of legs.

Crossing legs away from another person

When you cross your legs, you can choose to have it done with the legs away from the person you are dealing with. This sends a harsh message. This means you are not interested in whatever he or she is saying to you. It is a harsh way of showing disapproval and discomfort. Very few people have the confidence to tell people they dislike about their feelings towards them. If you are one such individual, then this positioning of legs might come to your rescue. There will be no need for additional talking to let such people read into your nonverbal communication. It says it all in clear actions.

Crossed legs when standing may indicate shyness

Crossing legs when standing may mean that the person is shy or is uncomfortable in a particular social situation. It may also mean that the person is tired of standing and wants to sit down.

Summary

Crossing the legs when seated is something most people do purely for comfort, especially women. But, sometimes it can mean that the person is feeling defensive or withdrawn or closed off.

Foot position is also a useful tool in body language interpretation. If the feet of the person are pointing at you when you are standing opposite one another, this indicates that the person is at ease with you. Their eyes will be focused on you and their head will be pointed in your direction.

However, if the person's feet are pointing in away from you, it is very likely that their head and eyes will also not be on you. This may indicate a lack of interest or a feeling of discomfort or awkwardness.

These are just a few of the tips that can be used for body language interpretation. Body language interpretation is a useful skill that you need to work on regularly. It is extremely beneficial if you know how to decipher the meanings of another person's body language. However, the indications are not true at all times. Not all impressions from reading body language last. This will only be supportive if you already have an idea on the personality of the person.

With more practice, you will be better and subtler in your approach.

Body Language Signals - Upper Body and Torso

Our arms and hands are another big key to body language interpretation.

- An open position of the arms portrays a feeling of honesty and that the person is accepting the situation.

- Crossed arms across the chest signifies a defensive posture, and it may also mean doubt or suspicion of what the other person is saying.

- Open hand palms express a feeling of being relaxed and comfortable.

- Putting the hands in the pockets is generally a sign of nervousness or lack of interest.

- The hands on the waist may indicate anger or fury.

  1. The way a person shakes hands can have all kinds of meanings:

  It's customary to stand up to shake hands. This shows a sign of respect. Eye contact held throughout the length of the handshake is a sign of sincerity.

2. The person who initiates the handshake is showing a sign of confidence, while sweaty palms indicates anxiousness or nervousness.

3. A Firm handshake with the hand pointing downward is universally recognized as a sign of confidence. The palms should also come in contact with each other. Too tight, it may mean they are overcompensating for something. On the other hand, a weak handshake with the hand pointing upward indicates shyness or nervousness.

Shoulders and Back

When the shoulders are squared and pulled back, without too much tightening of the back muscles; it indicates confidence.

When the back muscles are rigid and stiff, this indicates tension and nervousness. Slouching of the back or shoulders signifies laziness or boredom.

Crossed arms

There are several types of messages passed by crossing arms, but generally it portrays a defensive person. When you have arms crossed, it generally means you don't want communication with other people or external factors. Many people tend to pretend that they cross their arms because it is cold; thus would want to generate some warmth. In its shallowness, there are people who will interpret such an expression in a similar way. With due respect, this has a totally different meaning when it comes to dealing with body language.

It also implies that you are not ready to get engaged in any arguments or talks of that sort. This literally places a barrier on the front part of the body to warn any person with an intention of starting off a conversation. Therefore, you should be very wary about talking to a person who has crossed his or her arms. Vulnerability or a feeling of being insecure might inform the decision by a person to cross arms. If that is the case, it will be interpreted to mean that you are seeking self-comfort, and this will be necessary at such a point.

Whereas crossing of arms may mean one is closed to any arguments, there are additional signals that complete the gesture that you should as well lookout for. When a person crosses arms, he or she might complement that with a shake of the head to mean "no" or even avoid making eye contact by all means possible. Other signals might be the feet of the person pointing far away from your direction, crossed legs and leaning backwards. These are the signs you might see with a person who is crossing arms to keep people away.

Standing with hands placed on the hips

If you want to show the world that you are in full control of your life, standing with hands placed on the hips will be the right pose. People who know how to read body language well will tell you exactly that without misinterpretation. It can also be a show of aggressiveness. This pose is preferred most by men when flirting with women. They will tend to lean a little bit and that is interpreted to mean that the man is interested in a woman and would want to have her for another moment. This does not mean that women don't strike the pose. They do and it means the same thing. The pose can vary a lot but the constant factor is the hands on the hips. Anything else might change but that will not. The person might choose to lean forward while the head slides to one side. All that is meant to show attentiveness to whatever is being said and can be complemented by a simple smile and some direct eye contact. This is a pose of confidence and people who strike it are always ready to go to the extreme to achieve their goal. If you are aggressive and want to show it nonverbally, just stand up and place your hands on the hips. Everybody will be talking about you and your personality. It is more effective than walking around saying "I am aggressive". Always, actions speak louder than words and this body language fits the bill.

Clasping hands behind the back

Apprehension, frustration and anger are the main messages that clasping the hands behind your back will be sending to other people. It gives out the feeling of a person being naked and would not want to be seen by other people. Some discomfort might set in, which is the main sign of a person who is experiencing some anxious moments. You will feel like sitting down, standing up, walking and running all at the same time.

Expanding arms wide

Expanding your hands is yet another gesture that you can take to have the feeling of command. You will be trying to have as much space available for your use as possible. This is a gesture that will definitely boost your confidence because it marks out your territory. This is an effective nonverbal communication that will not need any words uttered to make people understand what you are feeling. Both men and women like taking this posture when they have some authority to command.

Another interpretation of expanded arms is preparation to embrace. This is more commonly seen by people who are about to hug each other. That is a very good way of showing affection to loved ones without essentially saying it. People hug each other as a way of greeting if it's not about affection; but will definitely send a different message if it involves those of the opposite sex. Even children embrace each other sometimes when playing, which should not be taken to mean too much of their actions. Expanding arms widely is a nonverbal communication that sends a strong message about ones' feelings.

Keeping arms close to the body

There are many instances in life when you will find it useful to keep your arms close to your body. Some sporting disciplines like golf and baseball lay more emphasis on the positioning of arms to cushion the body from injuries. That is one interpretation to have about this posture that also plays a vital role when driving a car. Apart from sports, keeping your arms close to the body can send a serious message about your inner self. It is a nonverbal way of communicating your emotions that many people have found to be useful.

This posture means you are keeping too much into yourself and would not want to attract attention from other people. Persons with this posture usually withdraw from the public to live a more private life, albeit temporarily. When you have some personal matters to handle and don't want interference from other people, just strike this posture and the message will reach them very well.

Rapidly tapping fingers or fidgeting

Are you fond of fidgeting or tapping your fingers rapidly? You might have done so on several occasions but not informed about the message you are sending across to other people. Those who are experienced in reading body language will easily tell that you are impatient, bored or even frustrated. That is one of the ways that people can release such tension from their bodies.

Body Language Signals - Face, Neck, Eyes

If you are interacting with a person and you are noticing him/her looking in the upward direction, do not worry. This gesture is often associated with thinking about a particular event or activity, being more common in those who are visual thinkers. However, when the respective person is also frowning, this might mean he/she is actually judging his/her interlocutor.

Public speakers often look upwards when delivering a presentation or holding a speech, this being a common gesture in such situations. It merely means that are actually trying to recall their presentation/speech. In general, if one is looking in the upward direction and to the left, this means he/she is trying to recall an event from the past. On the other hand, if one looks upwards and to the right, this means he/she is trying to imagine something, perhaps even a lie.

It is possible that the looking upward is an unconscious gesture, signifying that the person in question is bored. By looking upwards, he/she is actually examining the environment and tries to identify potential points of interest. The looking upward, combined with the slight lowering of the head, is a common gesture performed by people who are drawn to one another. By keeping your head down, you are showing yourself to be submissive, while the direct eye contact is a clear sign that you are interested in the respective person.

Eyebrows

Raised eyebrows express surprise or shock. A flick of the eyebrows while glancing at another individual shows that the person is acknowledging the other person or greeting him or her.

Nose

Touching or rubbing the nose is one of the most common self-touching gestures, which is usually done by people who are lying or trying to hide something.

Lips

Licking or biting the lips is one of the typical signals of flirting by women.

A kissing gesture can be done to show one's affection, and also used as a form of greeting.

Eye Movements

If the person has dilated pupils, he or she is interested in the conversation.

The eyes looking in different directions also have different meanings. When one looks up to the right, it means that he is imagining visual images. Meanwhile, when he looks up to the left direction, it means that he is trying to recall a memory. However, there are still instances where it is in a reversed order, depending on the person. Try to test him first by asking him to recall a known memory and to picture out an event.

On the other hand, looking down may mean that one is talking to himself, but this is more evident if there is also movement of the lips. It is also a potential signal of shame, guilt or submission. When people look down, it typically means that they are accessing how they felt about something. Looking down on another person means that he is control of the situation or is talking to someone who is under his superiority.

Lateral eye movements can indicate signs of dishonesty, distraction, or it could be that that are recalling auditory information. When looking from one eye to the other then going up to the forehead, it means that you are looking at somebody with superiority. When going down to the nose, you are talking to someone within the level of your status. And when looking from one eye to the other and down to the lips, it indicates a sign of attraction or romance.

Happiness

Happy facial expressions are some of the easiest that you can recognize without difficulties. They are universal and consistently convey positive messages. A friendly person will always have expressions of happiness on the face. Approaching such an individual will be very easy. It is said that facial expressions for happiness are more practiced than genetic.

This is because people tend to use them to hide negative emotions they might have in their system. Scientists have actually proven that some people have friendly expressions on the face but they are not happy inside, which is commonly known as "fake it till you make it."

Sadness

These expressions come as a direct opposite of happiness and will be seen in people who disapprove of anything. Such facial expressions will be seen in people who are mourning, going through any form of loss, those in pain as well as people who are generally uncomfortable with life. Unfortunately, there are some cultures that prohibit people from publicly showing signs of sadness on their faces, which is retrogressive. Such expressions come out of emotions, thus nobody can control it. The highlight of a sad face is crying, but there is big debate on that. This is in the light that tears do not necessarily say somebody is unhappy. There are tears of joy as well so you must be very precise in labeling ones face as sad by just looking at tears.

Anger

If you are angry, the facial expressions will say it all without your mouth saying anything. Anger is very common nowadays, as people vent out their annoyance caused by stress in life. If you are frustrated at work, in school or even at home, the end result will be anger. As much as you might try to conceal that from other people, your facial expressions will definitely betray you. Anger can result from both personal and interpersonal interactions. These facial expressions are more visible in personal interactions while interpersonal interaction seems to vent its anger in a more violent manner. You will find it easy trying to hit the person who is responsible for your anger. It is uncontrollable, but personal anger can be easily controlled. If it is not managed at the earliest opportunity, anger can result in conflicts. It is believed that anger expressions in men and women are different, but nothing tangible has been tabled to support the argument.

Surprise

How do you react to a surprise? Every person has a unique way of such reaction. Women are better known to prefer surprises (especially from their male counterparts) and their reactions are crazy to say the least. Some scream loudly while others jump up with joy - if it's good. However, surprises can be good or bad; so you must be in a position of differentiating between that. If there are any facial expressions that give people a hard time detecting or even taking record of, they are surprises. This is because they come unexpectedly so nobody is prepared. Also, they are generally short-lived, so there is no time to analyze them or take stock of what has happened. Once a facial expression occurs in response to a surprise, there are other expressions that follow immediately. For instance, if it's a bad surprise then an expression for sadness will follow. In case the surprise is positive then expect some expressions for happiness to follow.

Disgust

You will exhibit facial expressions for disgust once the body is subjected to anything that is nauseating. This can be as a result of a foul smell coming from something that is rotting, or even something bad you come across in your food or drink. These are generally expressions to show total rejection of something that is not welcome in your life. In many cases, people who show expressions of disgust on their faces have very minimal control over the situation but do so to demonstrate their dissatisfaction. Up to six linear muscles are involved when these facial expressions are exhibited. Common signs to lookout for in detecting the expressions include a raised upper lip, a wrinkled nose bridge and cheeks that are raised high.

Fear

Fear grips people who don't have an assurance of personal security and their faces are among the first body parts to show that. The eyes will tend to open up more than it's normal while brows are raised up. The mouth can open slightly as well, with five linear muscles and one sphincter involved. When these expressions are visible on the face of a person, they tell of an impending danger or threat. There are very many factors that bring about fear in people, that you need to study well and understand them before making a determination. Some responses from the body are responsible for bringing about anxiety, which translates to a dampened mood. If such fear is prolonged, it can end up causing some health complications thus should be addressed as early as possible.

Confusion

The forehead and nose will be the main determinants of facial expressions showing confusion since that is where most of the action is emphasized. If confused, you will experience the two parts being wrinkled up or even an eyebrow being raised high. There could also be the possibility of having your lips pursed together. Confusion epitomizes a case of total misunderstanding and these facial expressions will come out of the effort to get such an understanding. Every person has the desire to gain understanding of situations and avoid confusion, but it will happen at varied levels.

Excitement

There are different facial expressions that can be used to describe the state of excitement in a person. All in all, this is more positive and it shows something good has happened. These expressions are accompanied by a smile with the mouth wide open to show consternation. When excited, the eyes will be wide open, with the eyebrows rising higher to punctuate the energy levels. One will always appear to be cheerful and lively when excitement has crept in and the body becomes generally impulsive to any activity.

Desire

This is the urge to achieve something in life, and facial expressions can illustrate that very well. The expressions will vary from one situation to another since there are many desires we have in life. Desire works well with focus so you will have your eyes focused on the thing that you want to achieve. You will have minimal blinking of the eyes to avoid being interrupted while the tongue might be moving from one side of the mouth to another. During such situations, you will have more of your brain energy dedicated to achieving your desired thing.

Contempt

These are facial expressions that show complete disapproval of something. It is one way of saying a big "no" to what somebody else is trying to put on you. When you have an expression on the face showing contempt, it will have three key features. One, your chin will be raised up thus making it very easy to look at the offender. A sneer is another of the expression that will show clear contempt and is punctuated by a smile. The other feature of facial expressions for contempt is a tightened lip corner that looks raised on one side of your face. Some of these signs are very clear and you will not need any complex ways to read them.

Regardless of the type of emotions you are going through within your inner self, there are many types of facial expressions that you will use to exhibit that externally. It is on you to know the best way for interpreting that correctly.

What signification does looking down have?

From the start, it is clear that looking down is a gesture of submission. It is as if you wanted to prove to the other person that you are not a threat, trying to establish a clear relation. Sometimes, it can mean that the person in question is feeling guilty. Paradoxically, there are some people who use this eye gesture, to dominate others and demonstrate their power.

Looking down and to the left is associated with people who are accustomed to talking by themselves. If you would pay close attention, you would easily discover that their lips are moving, only slightly. On the other hand, looking down and to the right is associated with the expression of personal thoughts and/or emotions.

Looking down can be differently interpreted as a gesture, depending on the culture to which one belongs. For example, in many Asian cultures, it is considered impolite to maintain direct eye contact. By looking down, you will have shown respect for the person standing/sitting in front of you.

And what about looking sideways?

Looking sideways is one of the most obvious gestures that a person will make, upon being bored. Basically, the person in question is looking for new points of interest, thus looking sideways. Sometimes, we may look either to the left or right, to ascertain where a certain distraction is coming from. This is actually an ancestral instinct; the brain tries to determine whether a potential threat is close by or if something of interest is about to happen.

In certain situations, looking sideways can signify the person performing the gesture is irritated. The direction in which we are looking is also important; studies have confirmed that looking to the left is associated with the desire to recall a certain sound, while looking to the right occurs whenever we are trying to imagine the respective sound.

The lateral eye movement can tell a lot about yourself

The lateral eye movement involves the movement of the eyes, from side to side, being different from the sideways looking gesture. This gesture is often seen in pathological liars, especially when they are trying to get out of a certain situation. People who discuss secrets or confidential matters might present this gesture as well, being shifty and concerned that someone might hear about their plans.

Gazing and glancing

Gazing is a common gesture and one that we perform on a regular basis. When a person gazes at another person for a prolonged period of time, it may mean that he/she is in love. The concentration on the person's entire body is associated with feelings of lust, while the special gazing at one's intimate areas is a clear sign that sexual interest is present.

It is common for persons of authority to use gazing, to convince others to take a certain decision. In general, this gesture is kept short but at a high level of intensity. From another point of view, gazing is a gesture that is unconsciously avoided by liars; this is because, the longer they maintain contact, the guiltier they feel. Glancing, on the other hand, is short by definition and, depending on the situation, it can suggest a wide range of things: desire, concern, interest in something forbidden, attraction and even disapproval.

Is eye contact a form of communication?

From what has been said so far, you probably know the answer to this question. Once again, depending on the situation and the people involved in this particular type of communication, eye contact can suggest interest in someone/something, love and even the desire to dominate.

In the majority of situations, we are not particularly aware of the exact moment when we are making eye contact. All we need is to be interested in what a certain person has to say, then eye contact will naturally follow. However, one of the most difficult things in life is maintaining eye contact for a prolonged period of time (most people prefer the shorter version, as it is more comfortable and easy to disentangle from).

The longer eye contact is maintained, the more threatened we will actually feel. As an instinctual form of protection, most people will initiate eye contact, taking short breaks from time to time. Nevertheless, you must always pay attention to the significance this gesture bears, as you might end up insulting the person standing in front of you. Only in the situation that there is romantic interest between two people, is the breaking of eye contact deemed as an acceptable gesture. From a completely different perspective, it is worth mentioning that people who are insecure generally avoid eye contact. Also, those who do not want to be persuaded by others, will resort to similar behaviors.

Cultural differences in Body Language

History tells us that people started to shake hands, to convey peaceful intentions to others (and also the fact that they did not hide any weapons). Today, the handshake has become a common greeting ritual, helping one demonstrate the present level of confidence. A handshake can provide a lot of information regarding the person in question, especially when it comes to how willing he/she is to allow someone else in his/her personal space.

Handshakes can either be too weak or too strong, each situation conveying a different message about the person shaking those hands. If the handshake is too weak, this means that the person in question is not confident enough, being anxious or nervous with regard to the current interaction. A handshake that is too strong can mean a desire to dominate or over-confidence.

Cultural differences influence the meaning of handshakes as well. For example, in European countries, it is customary for men and women to shake hands, either as a greeting or as a form of agreement for a certain decision. In the Muslim countries, such an interaction is forbidden and severely frowned upon. Once again, we return to the idea of cultural sensitivity. We must always pay attention to culture and decide in an instant whether a certain gesture is culturally acceptable or not.

In countries like India, there does not seem to be much of a requirement to maintain a personal distance. It is pretty common to stay at a close distance when communicating with someone; whether you are with a stranger or not. China is another country of the world where people are not very much concerned about personal distance when interacting. The personal distance they keep is less important than accomplishing the goal of the conversation and interaction.

The precedent of keeping a safe personal distance is also very common and widespread in the western world. Do you know that personal space also entails some touching? Yes, that is the case and it's taken very seriously in South American and Mediterranean cultures. In these cultures, the general belief is that a conversation can be enhanced if one person in the conversation touches another. Their connection will also be stronger. Those who don't touch their friends while conversing are taken to be cold-blooded. Over in the eastern world, touching a person as you talk is largely a taboo and doing such a thing is taken as an offense. Actions like patting somebody in the back or even on their arms are unacceptable.

Before you travel to such countries, it is advisable that you take the time to learn more about body language in that culture, and what is considered appropriate, especially for personal distance. Inappropriate body language may lead to you becoming perceived as a bad-mannered person once you do things to someone from that culture or background.

Whether it is more appropriate to stay closer or farther away, make sure to educate yourself on which distance is the most suitable for the culture of the people you will be communicating with. Personal distance is one of the most important aspects of body language and carries a lot of implications in nonverbal communication. Another important part of body language and communicating with people from different cultures is your handshake.

Body Language in different social situations

How to use your body and impress others with your confidence

If you want to impress others with your confidence, you can use your body language and convey such information in an efficient manner. Begin with your posture and stand tall, making sure that your shoulders are straight. Educate yourself to maintain eye contact, smiling as much as you possibly can (when appropriate). Gesture with your hands and arms, in order to emphasize your talking points. Pay attention to the tone of your voice, keeping it between moderate and low.

How to know when you are being defensive

If you are in a situation where you feel your opponent is stronger than you or overly aggressive, you might begin to act defensive (conscious or not). Your body will give out clear signals that you are being defensive and it is for the best to learn how to recognize them. For example, if you refrain from hand/arm gestures, keeping these close to the body, you are clearly defensive. Defensive individuals will have very few or no facial expressions. They will turn their body away from the interlocutor or prefer crossing their arms, as a gesture of refusing further contact. Very little or no eye contact will be made.

It is possible to become defensive upon having to negotiate a difficult business deal. Watch out for the above-mentioned signals, in order to make sure that you are not being too defensive. You can learn how to be more open, using your body language to convey your openness and receptiveness for the negotiation proceedings.

Body language and lack of interest

If you have ever spoken to an audience, you are probably aware that it is extremely difficult to keep people engaged for a certain period of time. On the other hand, if you have ever been part of the said audience, you have probably shown this lack of interest yourself.

When you are not engaged in a conversation, discussion, meeting etc, your body will show this. The head will be kept down, with the eyes trying to focus on other things. You might spend your time picking imaginary lint from your clothes, playing with your pen or doodling. The posture is also a good indicator that you are not interested in the things being discussed, especially if you are slumped in the chair.

Your body language can say whether you are truthful or lying

A wise person once said that, if you want to find the truth, you have to analyze the body language of the speaker and now the words coming out of his/her mouth. People who are lying will maintain little or no eye contact, being agitated and constantly touching their face. They might also present rapid eye movement, as they avoid the focus on a particular individual.

It is common for individuals who lie to cover their mouth with their hands or fingers. They have an increased breathing rate, with their face and neck area being red in color. Perspiration might be presented in increased volume, while one might stammer or feel the constant need to clear his/her throat.

Body speaks before words

Let's say you are at an interview, for a new job. The interviewer asks you a difficult question and you are not sure about your answer. Before you speak, your body has already delivered plenty of information about your uncertainty. For example, you will avoid direct eye contact, while you are thinking about the answer. You might use your fingers to stroke your chin, touch your cheek with the hands and tilt your head, while your eyes look at the ceiling.

How to use your body to be more open and receptive

In order to show your openness, try a relaxed posture, with the shoulders kept in a straight position. This will show that you are confident and comfortable at the same time. From time to time, break your speech with a pause, as this will attract the interest of the interlocutor. If you also lean in, the success of the interaction is guaranteed. However, you need to make sure that you are not in the other person's intimate space, as you might be perceived as aggressive.

Try to maintain a wide support base, as this is a sign of confidence and openness. Refrain from leaning away from the interlocutor, as you will definitely be interpreted as hostile. Avoid crossing your arms and, instead, keep them in your lap or on the lateral of the body (signs of openness). If handshaking is necessary, go for the firm kind, avoiding the "crusher". Always maintain eye contact but watch out for the intensity (no staring).

When speaking to a large audience, it is highly important to remain just as open. For example, you have to remove any physical barrier, in order to ensure a sense of connection between you and the audience. No matter how uncomfortable or uncertain you might feel, refrain from crossing your arms, as this will establish a clear barrier.

From what has been said so far, you have probably understood that cultural differences have a clear influence on one's body language. This is even more valid when it comes to the social distance one deems as acceptable. First and foremost, there is the intimate distance, which is of only 45 cm. Only close acquaintances and friends are generally accepted at such a small distance. The personal distance is between 45 cm and 1.2 m, being used for meeting new people. From this distance, you can shake hands and realize a quick analysis of the other person.

The social distance, between 1.2 and 3.6 m, is the one commonly used between individuals for less personal interactions. Social distance is considered acceptable for business transactions and negotiations. In such situations, it is recommended that one speaks in a higher voice and tries to maintain eye contact at all times. Last, but not least, you have the public distance, between 3.7 and 4.5 m, which is used by teachers and other public speakers. At this distance, one will derive more information from the gestures made with the hands and arms, as well as from the movements of the head. The facial expressions of the public speaker are not that important, as they are not as well perceived by the audience.

Conclusion

We use our body language unconsciously. It transmits a lot of information about the way we feel and think. As you have seen in this book, body language accounts for almost all communication that takes place between humans. It entails facial expressions of the most varied kind, gestures that are common and rare, plus a wide range of highly suggestive postures.

From everything that has been written, you have probably understood that our emotions and thoughts are vividly expressed through non-verbal signals. Sometimes, we fail to perceive these signals, due to our cultural differences. In such situations, it becomes essential to become aware of cultural sensitivity and try to place ourselves in the other person's shoes.

We use gestures to tell others that we like them and we welcome them into our personal space. At the same time, we have a wide range of other gestures, reserved for those who do not like and clearly do not want intruding into our personal space. Handshaking is more than a gesture used for greeting, having a myriad of significances, as you have probably noticed. Smiling and laughter can ensure a successful interaction, suggesting to the other person we are alright and comfortable with the said encounter.

Always remember that your body has its own voice and that you can educate that voice, in order to convey the right information. Do not be afraid to learn about deceitful communication and how to identify the non-verbal signals other people use when lying. Respect the other person's intimate space and maintain eye contact, whenever you are interested in a certain someone.

The end… almost!

Reviews are not easy to come by.

As an independent author with a tiny marketing budget, I rely on readers, like you, to leave a short review on Amazon.

Even if it's just a sentence or two!

So if you enjoyed the book, please head to the product page, and leave a review as shown below.

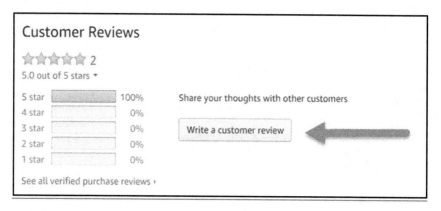

I am very appreciative for your review as it truly makes a difference.

Thank you from the bottom of my heart for purchasing this book and reading it to the end.

CPSIA information can be obtained
at www.ICGtesting.com
Printed in the USA
LVHW080138290520
655841LV00012B/194